THE CLIMATE CRISIS IN
THE SOUTHWEST

by Brienna Rossiter

FOCUS
READERS®
NAVIGATOR

WWW.FOCUSREADERS.COM

Focus Readers is distributed by North Star Editions:
sales@northstareditions.com | 888-417-0195

Produced for Focus Readers by Red Line Editorial.

Content Consultant: Douglas Kenney, PhD, Director of the Western Water Policy Program at the University of Colorado Boulder Law School

Photographs ©: Shutterstock Images, cover, 1, 8–9, 11, 18; Rick Bowmer/AP Images, 4–5; Phil Millette/US Fish and Wildlife Service/NIFC, 6; Red Line Editorial, 13; Natural Hazards/USGS, 14–15; Southwest Biological Science Center/USGS, 17; Felicia Fonseca/AP Images, 21; iStockphoto, 22–23, 25; Lauren B. Smith/Danita Delimont/Alamy, 27; Ross D. Franklin/AP Images, 29

Library of Congress Cataloging-in-Publication Data
Library of Congress Cataloging-in-Publication Data is available on the Library of Congress website.

ISBN
978-1-63739-636-0 (hardcover)
978-1-63739-693-3 (paperback)
978-1-63739-801-2 (ebook pdf)
978-1-63739-750-3 (hosted ebook)

Printed in the United States of America
Mankato, MN
082023

ABOUT THE AUTHOR
Brienna Rossiter is a writer and editor who lives in Minnesota.

TABLE OF CONTENTS

CHAPTER 1

Dangerously Dry 5

CHAPTER 2

Typical Climate 9

CHAPTER 3

Many Impacts 15

THAT'S AMAZING!

Navajo Water Project 20

CHAPTER 4

Solutions 23

Focus on the Southwest • 30
Glossary • 31
To Learn More • 32
Index • 32

DANGEROUSLY DRY

In January 2020, states in the Southwest faced extreme dryness. Water levels in rivers and lakes dropped. Temperatures soared. The hot, dry weather fueled wildfires. In Colorado, huge fires burned. Many homes and forests were destroyed. Smoke from the fires spread hundreds of miles. It made the air unsafe to breathe.

By 2022, water levels in Utah's Great Salt Lake had reached all-time lows. Some docks were left without water.

In 2020, the Cameron Peak Fire and East Troublesome Fire became the two largest wildfires in Colorado history.

The dry period lasted through August 2021. It was the region's worst drought since 1895. Scientists linked the extreme conditions to **climate change**.

In addition, Lake Mead and Lake Powell were drying up. These are the two largest **reservoirs** in the United States. In 2021, they reached record lows. Some people had their water supplies cut off.

In 2022, most of the Southwest became extremely dry again. Rivers and lakes dropped even further. The region faced even worse water shortages.

News outlets called both dry periods *droughts*. This term wasn't wrong. The periods were drier than normal. However, the Southwest has been getting drier since 2000. So, the droughts were part of a longer trend. Scientists did not expect that trend to stop. Instead, the Southwest was becoming permanently drier. This process is called **aridification**. Climate change was the main cause.

CHAPTER 2

TYPICAL CLIMATE

The Southwest's climate is warm and dry. However, the amount of **precipitation** varies. This difference is partly from El Niño and La Niña. These weather patterns are based on the temperature of the Pacific Ocean. El Niño happens when the ocean is warmer. It brings more moisture to the Southwest.

Climate describes long-term weather patterns. For example, a desert may have rainy weather one day. But its climate is still dry.

When the ocean is cooler, La Niña makes the Southwest drier.

Conditions also depend on location. The region has deserts, plains, plateaus, and mountains. As the elevation changes, the climate does, too. Elevation is the height of land compared with sea level. The southern part of the region has hot, dry deserts and plains. The plateaus tend to be cooler and rainier. They are higher up and farther north. The Rocky Mountains are even higher and cooler.

The Southwest is the driest and hottest US region. As a result, water is often in short supply. Much of the region's water comes from snowpack. This snow builds

Utah's Canyonlands National Park is in the Colorado Plateau.

up in the mountains during winter. Then it melts in the spring. It flows down from the mountains. It fills lakes, streams, and rivers.

The Southwest's climate has also varied with time. Scientists have tracked average temperatures and rainfall over the past 100 years. Some wet or dry periods last for decades. From 1905 to 1930, the region was much wetter than usual. But it was very dry from 1942 to 1956. This variation has been happening for many years. The Southwest had a series of huge droughts between the years 1000 and 1450.

CLIMATE TRACKING

Some scientists use computers to track and study climate conditions over time. This practice helps them learn what changes are and aren't normal. Scientists use particular methods for studying recent years. For example, they might use data collected by weather stations. However, methods are different for studying the more distant past. Then scientists might look at tree rings. Trees grow new rings each year. During wet years, rings are wide. Rings from dry years are narrow.

However, recent years are outside the usual range. The Southwest has had more heat and less rain than ever before. Climate experts say these changes are caused by human actions. **Greenhouse gas emissions** are the main cause.

THE SOUTHWEST

Great Salt Lake

Rocky Mountains

Salt Lake City

Colorado River

★Denver

UTAH

Colorado Springs

COLORADO

Lake Powell

Lake Mead

Colorado Plateau

★Santa Fe

ARIZONA

Albuquerque

Sonoran Desert

Phoenix

NEW MEXICO

Tucson

Rio Grande